LE NOVELLE DELLA C

Dante for Fun
The Paradise

Text by Cinzia Bigazzi

Illustrations by Valentina Canocchi

federighi editori

Text by
Cinzia Bigazzi

Illustrations and graphic project by
Valentina Canocchi

Executive editor
Gloria Pampaloni

Printed by
Federighi Colorgrafiche
50052 Certaldo (FI)
www.federcol.it

www.federighieditori.it
info@federighieditori.it

Translation by
AN.SE - Colle di Val d'Elsa (SI)

ISBN 978-88-89159-45-3

At last I had reached Paradise, which shone with the power of God. Beatrice, standing next to me, looked up at the sun, staring at it. All of a sudden, the daylight seemed to be twice as bright, as though God had decorated the sky with a second sun. Divine music filled the air.

Beatrice, seeing that I looked lost, explained:

"You're no longer on Earth. You're drawing nearer to God faster than lightning. Don't worry, all souls cleansed of their sins tend to rise upwards. Now we've reached the first of the nine heavens of Paradise, that of the Moon".

It felt like I was entering a luminous cloud, thick, consistent and smooth, like a diamond lit up by the rays of the sun. At a certain point I caught a glimpse of some spirits, but they were very confused figures, like reflections in glass. I turned back to see if there was anyone there and Beatrice, smiling, said: "The images you see are souls. Talk to them if you like, they'll be happy to answer".

So I spoke to the soul who seemed most willing to talk:
"Oh blessed spirit, enjoying the sweetness of eternal life, please tell your name and your story".
"Do you recognise me?", replied the soul, "I'm Piccarda Donati.

I became a secluded nun when I was just a young girl, but my brother Corso arranged for me to be kidnapped from the convent and forced me to marry a violent man and I died soon afterwards from the pain.

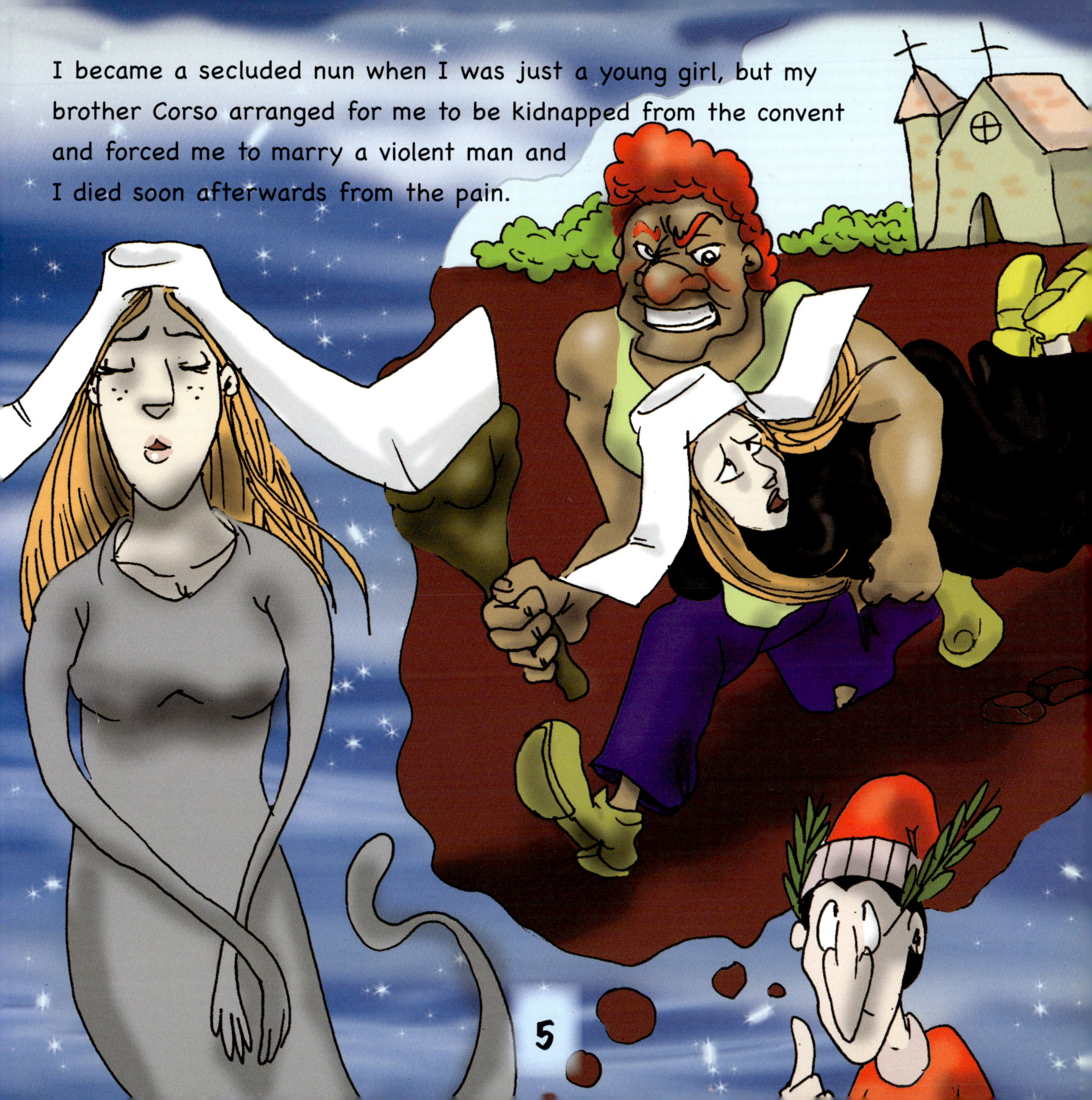

Now I'm in this heaven with other souls who have failed to keep the vows they have made".

Piccarda! I clearly remembered the story of that sad young woman, sister of my friend Forese Donati whom I'd met in Purgatory.

"Tell me, Piccarda, wouldn't you like to be in a higher Heaven, to be nearer to God?"

"Brother", replied Piccarda laughing happily, "our peace is in the will of God and the joy of all the skies is equal". As soon as she'd finished speaking, the spirit began singing the Ave Maria and vanished while she sang.

I turned towards Beatrice, but she blazed with such a bright light that I had to bow my head.

Then, as fast as lightning, we rose to the Heaven of Mercury, where we were met by a multitude of shining spirits, one of whom said to me: "O spirit, born to be good, divine grace has allowed you to rise up to heaven! Ask us what you wish and we shall be glad to answer".

"Tell me, oh kind spirit, who you are and why you are here", I asked that blessed spirit.

"I was an emperor and my name is Justinian. I entrusted my army to the valorous Belisarius and I devoted my time to reorganising the ancient laws of Rome. You ought to know that this heaven hosts those who, like myself, have worked to create works that would stand the test of time...".

I looked at Beatrice and her face seemed
to be lit up by a light that made
her look even more beautiful.

Without even noticing, I had climbed to the next heaven, that of Venus.
Here I found myself surrounded by lots of little flames, dancing and singing Hosanna.

One of them approached me, saying: "We are ready to fulfil your every desire, ask us whatever you wish and we will be happy to interrupt our dance and spend some time with you".

"Who are you?", I asked the spirit.

"I am Charles Martello, son of King Charles II of Angiò. I died when I was just 24, but if I could have become king of Sicily and Naples in place of my brother Robert, there wouldn't have been that terrible war of the Vespers down there...

Robert was as cruel and merciless as I was passionate. This sky is inhabited by spirits who loved purely. You might be wondering how two brothers can be so different: it all depends on the celestial influences, which convey a certain type of nature to each person. On Earth unfortunately, no-one takes this nature into consideration and it often happens that someone who should really have become a soldier becomes a priest, while someone who should have become a preacher is crowned King.".

After talking to this spirit, almost without realising it, I found myself in the Heaven of the Sun. Here the souls shone with such bright light that they stood out against the brightly blazing sun. They were the spirits of philosophers and scholars who had devoted their lives to investigating the mystery of God.

They formed a sort of crown, which moved around us, singing and dancing. Then those blessed souls stopped for a moment and one of them said to me:
"You who have been granted divine grace to climb this far, talk to us! I am Thomas of Aquinum.

while the man on my right was my teacher Albert the Great, that is the wise King Solomon and many others earned and wise men dance with".

"You know,", he continued, " Providence has established that two great men should come into the world: Saint Dominic, to keep the Church safe from the heresies, and Saint Francis who, practising humility, would have kept the Church's love of Christ alive.

I am going to tell you about the latter of the two. Born in Assisi, and son of a rich merchant, Francis could have lived a life of luxury. Instead, while still a boy, he chose to reject his father's wealth and began living in extreme poverty, preaching contempt for material goods.

Many people followed him.
Years later he withdrew to Mount Verna, where he received the stigmata.
When he sensed that death was near, he asked his brothers to bury him in the bare ground".

As soon as he had finished speaking, the crown of spirits began to revolve again.

At a certain point I felt myself carried upwards. I looked at Beatrice, who was even more beautiful and smiling: we had climbed to the Heaven of Mars.

Two rows of luminous, reddened spirits moved, forming the shape of the cross, with a flashing image of Christ in the centre.

One of these spirits broke away from the cross and came towards me:
"Oh my blood, I've been waiting for you: I read of your coming in the great book of destiny". Filled with amazement I exclaimed: "Blessed soul, shining like a jewel, please tell me your name".
"I am your great-great-grandfather, my son was the first of the Alighieri family:

born in Florence and named Cacciaguida, I left on a crusade to take the land where Christ was born from the heathens and lost my life in battle. This heaven is occupied by all those who, like me, died for their faith". "Oh dear root of my family! You who read the future in God, tell me, what awaits me in the days ahead?"

"You shall leave Florence and live in exile. You will know how hard it is to live thanks to the hospitality of others, but do not hate your fellow citizens because your glory shall remain in time and your enemies shall be punished".

"I see clearly the sad destiny that awaits me, but I will know how to proceed. Tell me though, can I tell of everything I have seen during my descent into the Inferno, climbing Mount Purgatory and passing through the luminous rings of heaven,

or would it be better to keep certain truths hidden to avoid provoking the anger of certain people?"
"Only those with a guilty conscience", replied Cacciaguida,

"will feel offended by your words, but you must tell of everything you have seen and heard".

After saying these words, Cacciaguida returned among the other lights of the cross and began singing with them again.
While I listened, moved, to that sweet melody, I turned towards Beatrice and saw that her eyes had become even brighter and she was even more beautiful.

We had climbed to the Heaven of Jupiter, where the reddish light of the Heaven of Mars had been replaced by a pale, white light. Here the souls sang and flew, happy as birds, and, with their flight, formed an eagle which shone like a ruby struck by sunbeams.

I asked them to dispel a doubt which had always troubled me:
"Tell me, blessed spirits, does it seem fair to you to lock out of Paradise upright men simply because they have not been christened?"
Altogether, the souls replied: "How can you mere mortals judge divine justice?

The will of God is love and on Judgement Day you will see how he punishes and rewards.
Remember, however, belief in Christ is not enough, you also need to act well! Now look me in the eye", said the eagle once more, "and you will see the spirits of the great, just men who have lived on Earth".

I saw the shining face of King David, Trajan, Constantine, William the Good and Ripheus.

I turned towards Beatrice, but she was no longer smiling: "If I were to smile", she explained, "you would turn to ash, because my beauty becomes more and more shining the further we climb. Now we have risen to the seventh splendour, to the Heaven of Saturn. Closely observe the things that appear before you".

Then I saw a golden stair which climbed so high that my eyes could not see the end. Lots of shining souls walked up and down it; one of them came towards me, saying: "Ask what you wish".

I plucked up my courage and asked: "Why is everything silent in this heaven, with none of the sweet songs that fill the other Heavens?"

"Your hearing is that of a mortal, so you would be unable to put up with that sweet melody.", replied the spirit, "I am Pier Damian. I lived in a lonely monastery among the Apennine mountains, immersed in prayer, until I was forced to become cardinal.

How times have changed! Saint Peter and Saint Paul were thin, they walked barefoot and lived on charity. Today's cardinals however are fat, they need someone to help them mount their horses and they wear big cloaks. How great God's patience must be".

In hearing these words, the shining souls on the stairs all shouted out so loudly that there are no words to describe the sound.

Afraid, I turned towards Beatrice who calmed me: "You're forgetting that we're in Paradise, where everything is good".
Then, with a simple gesture, she indicated that I should climb the stairs and, as though propelled by a wonderful force, I found myself in the eighth heaven, in the Heaven of the fixed Stars.

"Now we are close to God", said Beatrice, "There are the files of the blessed who were saved by Christ!", she added, her eyes filled with joy.
Suddenly a light which shone like the Sun appeared, with the image of Christ in the centre.
I felt as though I were losing consciousness due to the strength of that vision, but Beatrice encouraged me: "Open your eyes, now that you have seen these things, your sight has become so strong that you can bear my smile and the divine songs".

Then a light became detached from the others and came towards us. It was the spirit of Saint Peter. "Oh eternal soul", said Beatrice, "to whom God entrusted the keys to Paradise, ask this man with me about faith".
"Tell me, good Christian," said the spirit, "what is faith?"
"Faith is a gift of God which enables you to believe in the mystery".

Then the spirit of Saint James approached: "What is hope?"
"Hope is waiting for eternal life with faith", I replied.
Lastly, the spirit of Saint John arrived: "What is love?", he asked me "Love is the desire to move towards God, who is the beginning and end of all creation"."Holy, Holy, Holy", sang all the souls. I had passed all three tests.

I looked at Beatrice, the beauty of her smile now lifted me towards that heaven which is first moved by God, the Empireus, the heaven that does not move, which is pure light and joy. Before me there was a long river made up of shining lights between two banks covered with brightly coloured flowers. Sparks flew out of the river and rested on the flowers before returning to the river.

"The sparks you see are angels", said Beatrice "and the shining flowers are blessed".

Suddenly all those lights formed a ring, taking on the shape of a candid rose.

Angels with shining faces and golden wings descended onto the petals of the rose, like bees on flowers, singing Glory to God.

I felt lost, troubled by so much beauty, and I turned towards Beatrice, but she was gone. In her place there was an old man dressed in white, like the others who were blessed.

"Where is Beatrice?", I asked, worried.

"I am Saint Bernard of Chiaravalle and I will accompany you on this final part of your journey.

Would you like to know where Beatrice is? Look up and you will see her among the blessed of the rose", the old man answered softly.

I looked up and saw Beatrice, beautiful and radiant with joy in the middle of the blessed.

I offered her this prayer: "Woman, you who have restored my hope, I shall be forever grateful to you for what you have done for me". Beatrice looked at me one last time and then turned to face God.

"Now", said Saint Bernard, "watch the candid rose. Up there, among the blessed, you will see the Queen of heaven, the Madonna".
Indeed, I saw the brightest light of all, on which a thousand celebrating, dancing angels flew. In the centre was the Madonna. No words can express the delight which the beauty of Mary caused to flow in my soul.

San Bernardo also turned his gaze towards her and then offered her this prayer: "Virgin Mother, humble and merciful, grant this man the grace to see God...". The gentle gaze of Mary came to rest kindly upon me as though to indicate that the prayer had been accepted.

Then I saw God: three different coloured rings, all the same size. They were the Father, the Son and the Holy Spirit and in one of them I caught a glimpse of the human figure of Christ.

It was a fleeting moment, such a sublime vision that my mind is unable to describe it. I had become a new man, transformed by this great, divine journey. In my soul and my mind, now there was God, the love that moves the sun and the other stars.....

In my soul and
my mind,
now there was God,
the love that moves the sun
and the other stars.....